Smhaines1@gmail.com
www.SusanHaines.net

First Printing

This book is dedicated to my three children: Ryan, Heather, and Mallory. You have each been my inspiration and I love you circles and circles, never ending. In memory of my brothers: Mark and Mitchell, who no longer have their voice and to my sister Michele, who has always been there for me.

I would also like to thank my parents for giving me the opportunity to discover something more to life than what was and a big thanks to RL, for being the catalyst for my taking a new path in life. I am eternally grateful.

I *Married My Father* is my journey to self-discovery and to real happiness. I had lived my life for everyone else, trying to be a great wife, mother, daughter, and friend; never putting myself first. What this did for me was show me that no one really cared for me in the way that I thought they should. In reality, they never could because it is not their job to do so. Before this journey, I thought it was my husband's job to make me happy; I think that is the biggest misconception about relationships and marriage. Most go into relationships with unrealistic expectations and look back years later, trying to figure out what went wrong.

This book is my personal experience about how I found myself lost on a journey to nowhere and entangled in an unhealed emotional cycle that left me disconnected and numb. I had been there before, but this time I had no more to give and it was time to get in touch with my true self and break the cycle. This is my story, one of a woman trying to be what everyone wanted and losing herself in the process. This is an honest look at my truth through my memories, years of journaling, and reflection through my own eyes and feelings.

I MARRIED MY FATHER

Breaking the Cycle

by Susan Haines

TABLE OF CONTENTS

CHAPTER 1

WHAT MY FATHER TAUGHT ME

The phrase "daddy's little girl" is nothing new and probably is used in every household that has fathers and daughters under one roof! The media has their own distorted take on it as well; we see commercials depicting a father and his little girl playing in the park as he's pushing her on the swing. We then see her sliding down the slide into her father's arms. He lifts her up on his shoulder and the image fades to him walking her down the aisle. As we see the caption below, in a soft whisper we hear, "Where does the time go?".

I do believe this scenario is possible but it has not been my experience. I cannot say that I've encountered many girls in my life that have lived a fairytale upbringing, especially that of being a "princess." It is this mindset that disempowers women, as they believe that it is the man's job to make them happy. As such concepts are perpetuated in our society we will forever find women looking outside of themselves for happiness. I think it is great that fathers want to love their little girls and hold them in such high regard. But, as I take a closer look, in my personal opinion I feel the princess complex does more harm than good. Not to mention the men that will now have to try to fill daddy's shoes in maintaining this idea of specialness. I believe this sets women up for failure; the responsibility for all their needs is then put upon the unsuspecting, unfortunate potential husband. I am in no way implying that all little girls will behave in this manner but for the sake of argument, I am addressing the stereotype that is implied by the use of the word "princess."

It is safe to assume that the purpose of parenting is to teach by example. It is the parent's opportunity to share with their children what a healthy relationship looks like. The father will be the little girl's first impression of a man. The mother will be the little boy's first impression of a woman. In an ideal world both parents are emotionally balanced and are up for the task. In the defense of parents, if we did not learn this from our parents, then more times than not, we will be unaware of what our child needs. We may decide to parent differently or we may do the very thing that was done to us.

I can say, for me, that being a "princess" or "daddy's little girl" was not an option. I remember being very intimidated by my father. I was more interested in hiding, staying out of my parent's way. I knew enough about my father's temper to get out of dodge. His behavior was unpredictable, and we did not know what kind of mood he would be in before walking through the door. This put us on high alert. The moment we would hear him pulling in the driveway, everyone would scatter; we would find something to do. I saw his anger and how sometimes even the wrong tone, outfit, or something not done to his satisfaction could make for a horrible evening. My brothers typically got the brunt of his bad day. By the grace of God, my father did not physically abuse my sister or I. But the emotional abuse was just as damaging. The feeling of fear would fill my body as I witnessed my brothers being beaten and degraded for just being someone that he could bully. I remember my older brother running into a sliding glass door as my father was chasing him. There are too many stories to share about the level of aggression displayed by my father on a regular basis. However, this gives you some idea of the abuse we witnessed and my brothers endured.

At an early age, I became extremely intuitive in knowing the signs that became patterns of both my parent's behavior. I went undercover or invisible when possible. If getting tucked away in my room with my sister was not possible, then we would keep moving, staying, or at least trying to look busy. I made good grades in school. It was very easy for me, I now realize that I did this to get my parents attention. Looking back, when I got my father's attention it felt horrible because it was always after he had been drinking and he would praise me at my brother's and sister's expense. The attention I received for that did not feel right to me. As one child was built up, the others were taken down for not being able to achieve the same accomplishments.

My parents provided for us to the best of their ability. My mother was a fantastic southern cook and prepared four course meals every night. She was also an amazing seamstress and made a portion of my clothes when I was younger. My father was an underwater cable splicer for a large corporation and traveled extensively to places like Antigua, Barbados, Eleuthera, and Puerto Rico, just to name a few, sometimes weeks at a time. This created much stress for my mother, as she worked a full time job and handled all the other family matters that would arise in my father's absence. I remember her having a quick temper at what would seem like small things at the time; I now understand the stress in which she lived. I remember when my father's dad passed away. My father made the decision to leave his secure job, to work in the family business with his twin brother, raising pigs and cattle on the family farm. It was at this point I saw and felt the shift in not only my dad but also our entire family's level of dysfunction.

The craziness accelerated as my dad worked from sun up to sun down, six to seven days a week. It was physically demanding work and left him with nothing to give anybody at the end of his day. If I am honest, he did not have much to give before he went into the farming business. We never actually lived on the farm, my grandparents did. The drinking daily was obvious and sometimes would start before he would get home. My siblings and I just wanted to matter in our parents' eyes. The emotional support you think would be the most natural part of parenting in our case was non-existent. What were we to do when craziness was happening all around us and the two people that we looked to for comfort, emotional security, and nurturing were the source of the chaos and craziness?

I now see that my parents did not have the capacity to show us affection, no one had taught them how. Their parents did not give it to them, so they were in their own cycle. Once they became parents they simply continued what was done to them. My grandmother on my mother's side had some beautiful qualities, but they were overshadowed by her bitterness and lack of compassion for my mother. My grandmother on my father's side was not affectionate. I cannot remember ever getting a hug from her or sitting on her lap. I remember every time I would go visit, Evangelist Billy Graham or a similar Christian program, would be playing on the television. Back then I did not put it all together. My parents just did not have anything to give me. I just thought that my father was a mean man and that my mother was always in a bad mood, she hollered at us often. As I got older, I was so aware of what I did not like about my parents' behavior towards us and even in their relationship toward each other. I thought I had it all figured out. I thought that I would never marry a man like my father. I thought that I would never be the type of woman that would stay with a man that would emotionally bully me around and abuse my children, as my father had my brothers. Who was I kidding? I soaked up all the drama from my childhood and both of my parent's behaviors like a sponge. I never once thought that I would be duplicating it in my own world.

In preparation of writing my story, there was no denying the correlation between my parent's life and my own life. The character traits of my father, I now recognize in the men I had chosen as partners. For me, I am much like my mother. She turned a blind eye to the level of emotional abuse that was inflicted upon the entire household. She lived her life in denial, with the hope that it would get better.

This is very familiar to me because in looking back I did the same thing with my own family. Although my husband did not physically abuse his family, the verbal abuse was just as damaging. I too believed that it would get better. I made excuses for his irrational outbursts; I had adopted my mother's willingness to tolerate the mistreatment and disrespect from the man in her life, my father. It wasn't all bad, I also picked up a few of the lovely things about my mother, her fierceness in the kitchen and her ability to dress a table for the perfect Sunday dinner, a spread that would make Martha Stewart proud!

It was as if I lived out the drama that I witnessed as a child, right down to my feeling the need to prove myself. I saw this behavior magnified in my marriage. I was so disconnected that I had completely shut down, thinking I would live out my life in this dysfunctional marriage. After all my parents are still married. I could see no way out; I thought it would be until death do us part. I needed to talk to someone so I found a therapist that would later become a lovely friend. She would often say, "when someone is in enough pain, it is then that they are willing to take the steps toward change or freedom." The pain for me became so real and consuming that I could no longer ignore it or pretend everything was okay. I had to get real with myself and the reality of my relationship. My first reality check came when I had to admit that I did not want to be the victim anymore. There was no moving forward without changing how I saw myself. If we are to "break the cycle," we must realize that we have to start somewhere. How we see ourselves sounds so simple, but in truth it took me years to find Susan.

This chapter's title seemed so fitting because at first I thought what my father taught me was the value of hard work. What I remember of my father in years past was him working his tail off for endless hours. So that would surely be the value of hard work...right? Yes, he worked hard, but he expected everyone around him to do the same at all times. Sitting around was a sign of laziness, so if he jumped, we jumped. But, it was never enough or done to his satisfaction. As a teenager, I remember choosing to go out with my friends one night, without vacuuming my room first. When I returned home, I found that my father had put the vacuum under the covers in my bed as a clear reminder of his expectations.

My father was a tall man at 6' 7" and could be intimidating; no question he ruled the roost. I had no voice because you learned to agree or not say anything at all in the face of someone being a bully. So what I learned was to not honor my feelings, to have no opinion, to withhold affection, to feel insecure about myself, and to not trust myself. These things were not done intentionally but we truly are a product of our environment. I'm sure if I were to ask my father if he wanted me to grow up and marry a man like him, the answer would be no! This tells me that he did not have the emotional tools or willingness to change. He was repeating what had been done to him and did not choose to do it differently. I'm not sure if he knew that it was an option.

It is not what happens to us, but what we do about it that makes the difference. I knew that I wanted my children to have a voice and to feel wanted and respected. I wanted to do things differently and for the most part I did. I love my parents but there are many things that neither of my parents recognized in our upbringing. When something is said by any of us in present time, it is made light of as if it was nothing, or laughed off, which only shows me their hidden pain. Growing up, if I had not been around both sets of my grandparents and saw first hand the lack of emotion and nurturing that was shown to my parents, it would have been more difficult for me to forgive them for not being the ideal parents.

FINAL THOUGHTS

This is a portion of the process of a cycle unfolding. The beauty is that I am willing to live my life differently. I was in a daze for the majority of my life. I had never put the pieces together that my life was a direct reflection of what I had experienced as a child. The things that I disliked about my parents became the things I disliked about my husband and myself. I started to feel self-pity for the woman that was willing to take the bullshit from the man she called her husband. The man she was willing to do almost anything for. I wanted him to acknowledge me just for being the woman I was.

CHAPTER 2

HALL PASS

The term "hall pass" means many things to different people, depending on who you ask. For me, a hall pass takes me back to high school where you would do anything to get out of class and roam the halls! The teacher thought you were heading in one direction, but in fact you had another agenda.
Throughout our marriage, I gladly allowed my husband playtime with the guys, a night of cards or weekend excursions, simple trips, right? In my husband's case, simple turned into extravagant. A night of cards would turn into a weekend in Las Vegas. A fishing trip would mean a trip to the Bahamas in a 33-foot speedboat. I did this because I trusted my husband. He was a great provider. I knew that he worked hard and I wanted him to take time to enjoy himself with his friends. I never questioned anything; I trusted him completely.
I never thought that I had anything to worry about by giving my blessing to his weekend getaways. My thinking was that by me allowing him space would strengthen our marriage, when in fact it had the exact opposite effect. In my eyes, I thought the "hall pass" was a nice gesture, a way to let my husband know that I appreciated him for all of the hard work that he did for me and our family. But over time it went from his asking to go to becoming something that he was entitled to. I started to feel as though he was taking advantage of the situation. From there, it went from a conversation between the two of us discussing what he wanted to do to "oh by the way, I am heading to Costa Rica fishing with the guys on such and such a date."
It then got to the point where the trips were already booked and paid for before I even knew about them.
It never crossed my mind to fear him leaving with the boys or suspect any misbehaving. At times, he pretty much did whatever he wanted, whenever he wanted, with little or no consideration for his family. He started

to live his life as that of a single man and it appeared as if there was no care for anyone but himself. It is not that he abandoned us, but it was his emotional support and physical presence that we wanted more so than any material possession he could provide. But because he was a great provider, I think in his mind this made up for his getaways and lack of emotional support.

I wanted to ensure that my husband could focus on our business without any additional stress and I truly loved being able to help him in any way that I could. I have always loved spending time with my children, even in car pools! I did not want to be "that wife," nagging him the minute his feet hit the front door after a long day of work. Even though I felt depleted and drained after trying to keep it all together, I wanted him to be present when he arrived home and to be there for me on an emotional level, as I wanted to be there for him as well. I wanted this to be an opportunity for us to share our day and spend time together as a couple. On a typical evening, he would come home from a business trip or after a crazy day at work and there was nothing left for me except a couple of TV shows and him falling asleep in his favorite chair, totally exhausted. He did not give me the emotional support that I needed. It all sounded good for me to put the responsibility on him to take care of my emotional needs, but I now realize that it is something that I must do for myself. I was reaching out to be saved, but attempts to be a good wife landed me in a position of being unimportant in my marriage; I was replaced by other people and possessions. My willingness to go along with everything, when it came to my husband, created twenty plus years of a hall pass.

I knew that by keeping my feelings of disappointment

and suspicious thoughts inside that there would always be peace in our house. The more I held it in, the more outlandish his antics became. The thought of trying to keep the peace sounds great in theory, but the reality is it created an internal hell and I am the one that paid the price. I slowly started to lose my grip, my self-esteem, and my self-respect. Actually, it had all been nonexistent for quite some time. This then fueled my need to question everything about myself from my hair, clothes, to the color of my nail polish; I obsessed about every little thing! My biggest fear was his temper, it would get triggered if he felt cornered or drilled. He was clever in making me feel as if I had no right to question his comings and goings, often saying he was not my guy if I wanted a nine-to-five husband.

I hated that I had to ask for details when they could have been easily provided by him, out of respect for me. There were times when I would tell him all that had been bothering me, reaching down in the depths of my pain and I would summon all of the unanswered questions. All of my suspicion would well up in me and come out in a blade of fury. He was very good at double talking and would twist my words to the point that I would actually question what I had seen or heard. My words would come right back to me in a way that would make me feel stupid for even bringing it up. I did question my own sanity and I thought maybe he is right and I did not see or hear what I was so convinced that I had. As I look back it seems so bizarre that I even faltered on what I knew to be the truth.

It was when our business was approaching the heels of great success that I started to see a shift in my husband's demeanor. He began to act superior with a sense of entitlement.

There were countless times that we would be dining out with friends or family and the night would be ruined by my husband's behavior or inability to control his emotions/temper. It could be something as simple as the food taking too long to arrive or not prepared to his satisfaction. That alone could set the tone for the rest of the night. I have been so humiliated by his gross exaggeration of whatever the circumstance were at the time. This behavior would cause me to shut down because we were with friends or family. I had to put on the face and carry on like nothing had happened.

I started to see his true colors; it was not that this was new to me but the difference now is that it was more frequent and the delivery was much harsher. Each time I would lose a part of myself as I began to run out of excuses for his behavior. In those moments, I resented him and the person he was becoming. With the growth of the company, our family dynamics started to shift. There were fewer conversations about what I thought were our family goals and more talk about the business and employees. I saw our family unit being replaced by the company that had operated out of our living room in the early days. All of our conversations revolved around his work, the employees, and the big job deals that he was hoping to get. A few of his employees that he befriended on a personal level, would become his buddies on the weekend and back to employees on Monday. The lines between boss and employee always became blurred and left up to question. They became his family; in their eyes he was a big shot and in our eyes he was a husband and a father. His need to feed off being a big wig became more important than being, in his words, "a boring family man."

In the early years of the company, my husband would

take all of the employees on a three day cruise. This was done without spouses or significant others. This really bothered me, yet I said nothing. I started to feel resentment towards him and at times, I would be filled with so much anger that everything would come out sideways. I would walk around with an attitude and make snappy remarks about everything. At the time, I believe it was easier than just putting it on the table for discussion. The cruise, for many of the employees, was the first time that they had ever been on a trip like this and to not share it with their partners seemed so ridiculously wrong. I was able to stuff my unspoken words in the back of my mind as the trip came and went. But sure enough, the minute they hit solid ground the next cruise was in the works for the following year.

The following year, as the second cruise was rolling around, I became so jealous of the whole situation. Jealousy is defined as resentment against a rival and for me that was the company! My competition and my feeling of replacement in my mind was now the company. I detested the feeling of jealousy and what it brought out in me, it is not what I wished to be. It seemed to consume me and there wasn't much I could do; those were some difficult times. I was now in competition with my husband's work life; the office was his home and the employees became his new family. All of this only made me feel worse and I had to realize that I could not compete. The idea of them all going on another cruise again without spouses did not sit well with me and as I observed from a distance it looked and seemed like my husband was preparing for spring break. It was at this point, that I started to question everything. There was something different this time, but I still wanted to hold on to that trust even though his behavior reflected something completely different.

That was the turning point in my mind; I started to pay attention to every little thing. I felt like a private investigator and I hated every minute of it! The thing that I did not expect would eventually surface in my relationship. This was for me the ultimate betrayal in a marriage. Some things he confirmed and others he denied. It is not necessary to go into details because this is about my awakening to self-love. It is not about my husband's lack of interest in me and inability to be an honorable husband. It's more about him being the catalyst for my becoming courageous enough to be the example of a woman that demonstrates self-love and self-worth.

FINAL THOUGHTS

I know that it all had to unfold, as it did for me, to get it. It doesn't matter how long it takes, we will always get to where we are going. In the beginning, I had no idea that this is the turn my life would take, but I am grateful for the journey and I am looking forward to the next chapter, no pun intended. I now see that I have the power to live the life I desire to live, one filled with great love and joy filled days.

CHAPTER 3

WHAT MY GUT WAS TRYING TO TELL ME

For most of our lives, we hear trust your gut, your instinct, or your feelings. I knew clearly what this meant, but I just couldn't summon the power or clarity when I needed it most. For me, it was always in hindsight that things became clear and sometimes that hindsight took days, months, or even years. One experience comes to mind; As a young girl we lived in a rural area next to my grandmother. Between our two houses was a big open air shed. A teenage boy, probably around 15, lived near that shed. He coaxed me inside with the promise of some kind of treat. In the corner of the shed, was a stack of old tires, and he asked me to get in them. In that moment, I had a sense of trust at first and went with him, but when I got a closer look at the tires stacked up, it was a huge red flag. Regardless, I let him put me in the tires. It was then that it truly hit me, that this was not right and I felt a true sense of danger and needed to get out of there. I immediately said that I had to go home, that my mother would be calling me. I must have started to get louder because he allowed me to leave. I think it also had to do with the shed being between my house and my grandmothers. In any case, there was a distinct feeling of discomfort that inspired me to say those words and to speak louder.

I went through life with obvious signs of red flags, but I chose to look in the other direction. I thought that this would make the issues that I was trying to avoid disappear. Actually, this had the opposite effect and it was all brought to my doorstep. Although I was in denial, this didn't stop the drama from finding me.

My childhood was filled with chaos, anger, drama, and abuse. Trust me, those words are a mild description of the hell we endured. My mom was preoccupied with life and at times she would lash out at us as well. She was under a lot of stress and pressure and this alone was enough to set her off.

As kids, we played outside all day long. There was no in and out, grabbing endless snacks before heading back outside like my kids did. The times outside are some the best memories for me. I remember playing down by the lake, catching minnows, and making mud pies with my best friend, Sue, who lived next door. Again, busy was the key word here!
My dad was a functional alcoholic but when happy hour would roll around, you could feel the energy change. It was like living with Dr. Jekyll and Mr. Hyde. We were always walking on eggshells, for we had no idea who he would verbally attack or provoke with his prejudice, misguided beliefs.

Sadly, my two brothers saw the physical effects of his addiction most of the time. I can remember the feeling of helplessness when I would witness them being physically hurt or verbally brought down and humiliated. When you think of abuse or bullying, you think of physical violence, but I can tell you that someone can destroy a person's self-worth with his or her words. My older brother left home at 16. It was so bad that he slept in the woods across the street. I don't remember him moving back in with us. It did not seem to faze my father in the least that my brother was camped out in the woods. Once he was no longer living at home, it just left my younger brother Mitchell, whom I was very close to, and I. I always felt responsible for his pain and wanted to do something, but I was too afraid to speak up. There were times my sister, Michele, would say something, but it made no difference. I would get so upset I would just go to my room and cry. My mom would step in and that was even crazier because she would scream and shout at the situation, not backing down, and then be so upset herself. It became a predictable cycle. Even in her fit of rage about his abuse, she never left. It would happen again and again, more yelling, but nothing more was done.

Most of my adult life, I carried the burden for not standing up for things that mattered, but mostly for my brothers. In the midst of my upbringing, it is clear as to why I had no understanding about self-trust. The fact that I did not say anything may have been a blessing in disguise. I know that the feelings of guilt have shaped my life in ways that I could not have imagined. I became that person who wanted to make everything better for everyone, especially my family and more so my brothers. I carried the burden of others at the expense of my emotional and physical well-being. My life was filled with distractions, I responded to situations and relationships from a place of being disconnected. It was all fear and guilt based and I literally operated on autopilot! This cluelessness has given me new understanding of myself and of life.

My first husband was my saving grace to some normalcy, or so I thought. I was 18 when we met and after a couple years of dating we got married and started playing house. He worked nights and I worked days. For the most part, we had separate friends and did our own thing. I was in the work world, meeting all kinds of people my age that were enjoying life.

My husband was six years older than me and it was not long before I realized that the union was not genuine and again I was living with someone who liked to drink. Most of his down time was spent with my father, drinking beer and fishing. Years would go by before I would have the courage to ask for a change. The best thing that came of the marriage was the birth of our son.

I did not want to live the rest of my life without a true connection to someone; I wanted and needed to feel loved. I watched my parents for years argue and be so stressed out, yet every night like clockwork my mom would prepare an amazing southern meal and we would all sit down, to pretend all was normal. I knew this was not what I wanted. I wanted something different, I wanted to have the type of husband that would appreciate me and love me, for always.

As I am writing this chapter, I see the woman that I've become, which is the woman I saw as a little girl holding it together for those years for the sake of saving face, just like my mother. I now realize that the only way that anyone could exist in such an environment is to check out. It all made sense now; I had become my mother.

I finally worked up the courage to ask my husband for a divorce, which he did not take well. Due to his personality and his inability to see the need for this change, he checked himself into a treatment center for emotional health, where they prescribed a mind altering medication. Once he was out of the treatment center, he returned to working the night shift, while I continued to work during the day. After work, he would mix the medication with alcohol, making his behavior very unpredictable and destructive. Without too much detail, the home we shared was literally torn apart, while I had been working, room by room. One night I would come home to the plumbing ripped out of the master bedroom; the next day it was our son's bedroom. This was not normal behavior for him; I think the picture is clear of the seriousness of the matter and the increasing change due to the medication and alcohol.

With all of this happening, I still did not call the authorities. I was in such denial of how he was acting and what he was doing. I kept telling myself, "this is not him doing this." It just was not his personality. By this time, my son and I were living at my parents' house, for safety reasons. The next evening, I was awakened in the early morning hours with my husband standing over me asking me to come outside to talk. I followed quietly, not to wake up anyone in the house, including my sleeping son in the bed next to mine. Once outside, my husband pulled out a pistol and told me to get in the truck so that he could talk to me; without hesitation, I did what he said. Once in the truck, we went on a little ride, he spoke of many things. I later discovered, that everything he shared on that unforgettable early morning was untrue. The entire conversation was about him and his state of health. I was fairly sure I was not getting out of his truck in one piece but I did three to four hours later. After he dropped me back off at my parents, I calmly walked in the house and began to make a pot of coffee. Minutes later, my father walked in the kitchen, said "good morning" and asked what I was doing up so early. I told him about my last four hours, but I was torn because this was so out of character for my soon to be ex-husband. My father was surprised and in disbelief about his behavior. This was difficult for him to believe because my father and my husband were weekend fishing buddies up until all of this began.

I still did not call the police, even after my joy ride; crazy, I know but it gets better. The following night, I heard a loud noise and knew we had a visitor. I jumped out of bed, yelled for my father to get up, ran in the kitchen to dial 911. About that time there was banging on the side door, which went on until my husband appeared around the back of the house outside the sliding glass doors. I ran to my room where my son was and my parents stood in the kitchen. My soon to be ex-husband shot his pistol through the glass doors and was coming for me! The rest is a blur but the police surrounded the house and had both my father and my husband in handcuffs on the ground. They came back in the house and I opened the bedroom door to pistols pointed at my face. The sheriff's department did not know who was who in the house and had to be prepared for anything. There is more to the story, but the point is I did nothing even when my gut was screaming, "get help!" I started the process of getting a restraining order and that, in of itself, was so humiliating and degrading for me as a woman. The way the system treated me was like I had done something wrong. I believed that he would never do anything to hurt his son or me. He was a very kind person, he helped people and could do any type of handy work you needed. I never thought that the cocktail combination of pills, alcohol, and his inability to cope could completely change him.

Some of you may be reading this and thinking, has she lost her mind? What person in their right mind would take this? Well, I did, and then I took it again the next night. I felt extremely robotic in my actions and the whole time I never gave my son a clue as to what was happening. He slept through that horrible night and I told him that a bad storm had come and broken the glass doors; I never said a word to him about that night. I did not want to damage his view of his father, so I held it in for many years. About six years ago he asked me if there was something that happened in his childhood that he was not aware of and I just assumed that maybe he was awake that night after all. I told him the complete story from my memory. To this day, it has remained his choice as to what his relationship with his birth father would be.

These days, I am trusting, or I should say honoring, my gut. I have planned and held holiday gatherings for most of my adult life. I have experienced things at these dinners that would blow your mind. My sister and I have always dreaded the holidays coming knowing there would be some type of outburst that was sure to happen. We were never let down; there was always a show! The best part was the aftermath where everyone would pretend like nothing happened. "Who does that?" is now the question that comes to my mind. Well, I did, we did and we did it amazingly well year after year.

FINAL THOUGHTS

My faith has given me the courage to share my story and faith has given me courage to forgive my family and myself. I knew that I could do something different, that I deserved more and my children deserved more. It is when we are willing to tell the truth to ourselves that we have the opportunity to change or "break the cycle" of dysfunction and redefine what is possible!

CHAPTER 4

HONORING HIM MEANT DISHONORING MYSELF

Dishonor is a lack or loss of honor or reputation. I did not have a clue as to what was meant by self-honor. I feel as a wife, mother, sister and daughter that these things are unintentionally stripped away from us on a daily basis. Unfortunately, it is the world we live in, one that would have women believe they are the caregivers. We are conditioned to believe that everyone and everything must come before us. If we are fortunate, or unfortunate, to be married, depending on the man, the husband comes first. Most wives are expected to take care of the house and in this day and age, she is also expected to work, take care of the children, and finally herself, if she remembers. I know in some cultures women are treated much worse, in some cases they can't work or receive an education. But the message still implies that women are less than their male counterparts, that their contribution is less important and devalued. As the role of the mother, much is expected of her with the full sacrifice of self and her personal well-being.

As a child, growing up in a drama filled household, I watched my mother try and keep it together, with the stress of working a full time job and raising a family. It was all she could do to keep from pulling her hair out. She had no time to teach us about self-honor or anything else for that matter. My father was always away on work assignments and when he was home happy hour would creep up earlier and earlier, which only added to the level of chaos. I now believe that my mother did what she thought she needed to do to make sure that all our needs were met, including staying in a dysfunctional marriage.

I am truly a byproduct of my environment. These words reflect my life completely. My second husband was rarely home. If he wasn't at the office, he was at some type of event or trade show. When he came home at a decent time, he was usually too tired or preoccupied for quality time with me.

I don't think that he cared one bit about all that I had to do to run the house, not to mention making sure that the kids were looked after. I guess because he worked outside the home, my work inside the home was less important and more of something that was expected. In my desire to have some type of relationship with my husband, I tried to be the ideal mother and woman that he needed. I so desperately wanted him to notice me, to acknowledge me for just being his wife. My neediness stems from my being a little girl and wanting my father's approval. Since it was never given, I spent the majority of my childhood trying to figure out ways to get noticed. I can see that little girl, now grown up and still seeking approval from a man. This time it was from her husband. But, like my father, my husband didn't give it to me.

A part of me knew that my husband appreciated me, but he never said it. Again, if my father or husband were going to say something nice about me, it was never directly to me. It was always by word-of-mouth; it was never said in my presence. If there were any flattering remarks from my husband, I would hear them through the grapevine. At those moments I would be surprised because he was not in the habit of expressing the good that I was doing.

I believe that I would have a different story to tell had I been raised in a household where my parents expressed love for one another openly, in the way of showing affection. Not just between themselves but toward their children as well. Who knows the outcome of children brought up in an environment filled with love and support. It is not the material things that will shape the children's lives but the relationship or lack thereof that the parents have. In my case, I wanted to do it differently with my children. I wanted them to know that they matter to me and that I love and support them completely.

I accomplished this to a degree, but my teaching them about self-honor came at the price of a divorce. I could not have taught them this while being in a loveless marriage. There is no self-honor while suffering in silence. My children were at an age where they knew that something had to change, as was I, and this time I was willing to take the necessary steps to make it happen. There was no more fear, it was for my own sanity and desire to set myself free.

In my father's defense, I had the privilege and blessing to see into my father's childhood. I witnessed how my grandparents had treated their son, my father. It all made sense and it all came full circle. After observing this, my feelings towards him softened a bit, but the damage had been done. I know that everyone has the choice between what they feel is right or wrong. I am clear that my father knew the difference and yet continued to make the same choice over and over again, never taking into consideration what it was doing to his family.

With this said, it is never too late to change, to forgive, or to say I'm sorry. This is the opportunity for healing. The opportunity to break the cycle, to tell a new story. We must get to a place where we are no longer interested in disempowering another because of our own shortcomings. We then increase our chances to do the same from generation to generation. More times than not, we end up like our parents, or in my case marrying men just like my father. The things that I resented in my dad, I was attracted to in my partners. I eventually got to a point to where I was not comfortable being in the presence of men that disrespected me.

It started in my childhood as I watched my father disrespect my mother. I had no role models so I became what I saw and heard. I always thought I would not end up like that in my own household when I became a wife and a mother. I did not want fighting and belittling, truth be known, that was the reason I married the first time, I wanted to get away from the drama, only to run into the arms of more drama. This was the environment that I was most familiar with and so this was the life that I created for my children and myself. I was willing to do almost anything to save my marriage. This meant not saying what I was truly feeling and not verbally putting into words what I witnessed or saw; I did not stand a chance. I had no foundation so I was left on my own to navigate through the world and more importantly through adult and romantic relationships. Living a life from a dishonorable place opened the door to a life filled with countless opportunities to validate my insecurities. By the time I reached adulthood, I was willing and ready to do what was expected. Get married, have children, watching life go on and with every passing day I became more and more lost in chaos. This was the norm and disconnection became my daily routine.

Everyone in my life, present and past, has played an important role to my being the woman I am today. I do not look at my life from a place of blame and pointing the finger. It would be much later in life that I would start to listen to what my feelings and gut had been trying to tell me all along, that I can't look to anyone else but myself for change. "I am enough and I do matter!," words that I wanted and waited for my parents to tell me and when they didn't, I went to the men in my life to acknowledge me as a wife and mother, to put me before all others. The people that I looked to for the nurturing, love, and acceptance did not have it to give to me. The saying "you can't give what you don't have" is so true, but as a child what you are given is somehow enough or all that you think it should be. In reality, you come to expect nothing more, that is until you start to look within yourself. Now, I totally see the dysfunction of my childhood and how it affected me in both marriages. I was my mother and I had married my father, for he had all the traits of an unhealed man and no intentions in improving himself. Although I was not physically abused, the hurt and pain that I witnessed as a child became my own, it became my life.

FINAL THOUGHTS

I am no longer willing to settle for what was. Instead I am willing to grow and redefine my life in a way that empowers my children and I. I want them to know it is never too late to be the person you are meant to be. I wish to teach by example and revel in the joy of self-honor and appreciation. This is the gift to my family and friends, the gift of being my best self. I have my parents to thank, for if it wasn't for their behavior, I would not know what I truly deserve and what true self-love feels like.

CHAPTER 5

THE CALL BEFORE ME

I remember being in the delivery room, in labor, when my husband felt the need to take a phone call and he made light of it. I thought it must have been an urgent work matter and that my husband was so important that everyone needed him. There it was, right there before my eyes, the basis of our relationship. What I thought made him important became what he put in front of his family and myself. It was a relationship filled with everything but me, I was never an equal in our relationship and it was as if I didn't matter. To be honest, I was rarely included in any of the decision making and most things decided on I would find out after the fact. As I write these words I feel a sense of sadness for that woman. I think, "How is it possible that someone could allow herself to be treated this way?" When I look back, I can see how someone like her could find herself in such a predicament. Revisiting my past, I see the signs of the making of a girl that is disconnected. The level of unhappiness and disdain I felt towards my father, for instilling fear into the family, was more than I ever realized. This sent me running and jumping into a relationship with both feet, marrying with the thought of being rescued and getting me out of the house.

I now believe that my lack of emotional support and need for approval from my family and parents was the perfect combination for an inharmonious life. I wasn't aware of the effects of my childhood until I was in a relationship. In hindsight, all was made clear; I see what the lack of support did for my self-esteem. It sent me on a life long journey looking outside myself for approval. I needed the men in my life to validate me and to tell me how special I was. I didn't get it until much later in life that the men that I was looking to fulfill this void within me could not.

They never could because they did not give this to themselves. They also looked outside for approval. Whether it was taking the work staff on lavish trips, buying fancy cars, or to the bottom of a vodka bottle. It is all the same and comes down to trying to fill a void that can only be filled from within them. As I re-examine my life, I see the examples that were set for me by my parents. I'm not saying that it's the case for all of us, but definitely the majority. I now see the importance of being a good example for your children; they miss nothing. What they don't see, they hear. My parents were busy making a living and every obstacle in their life was dealt with through out of control arguments and my father taking out his unhealed pain on my brothers.

I am not sure to what degree my mother and father were abused and neglected, but the few stories of their childhoods that they have shared were harsh. I know it had to have been difficult for them. With that said, there is still no excuse for what we were subjected to. The sad part is that I never told my father how his behavior affected and shaped my life. I wasn't aware of the effects of my childhood until I started this journey. It wasn't until I was ready to take an honest look at my life, that the cycle would unfold.

I just wanted out! At the first opportunity, that's exactly what I did. I was free of my father's need for control and abuse, so I thought. The emotional fear, loneliness, sadness, helplessness, and unworthiness I experienced as a child were the tools I was given to build my life. It has become clear why I've lived the life that I have lived, after watching my brothers being abused and my parents arguing on a regular basis. I often wondered how my mother could have stayed in such a relationship and now I know. It's from being disconnected from self, having no self-worth, no self-respect, and no self-love. This had become the basis for tolerating the neglect in my relationships. The issue is not the fact that my husband would take a call, which I thought made him important, it was the fact that he made a choice as to what was important in his life and it was never me. I believe anyone that puts business before family, also puts their business before themselves. I've been guilty of it, putting all of my extracurricular activities before my own personal needs. This was a way that I could avoid my life. I didn't have to face the fact that I was unhappy. I didn't have to face the fact that I was in a relationship with a man that was unavailable.

There were times when we would take a family vacation and I would be so excited for quality time with my husband. But, within minutes of even getting on the road, he would take a call. When he was on the phone everyone in the car had to be quiet and listen to what was unfolding in the conversation. Most often, it was putting out a fire on a current job or company issue and sure enough, he would get angry and start yelling and cussing and the entire energy for the rest of the drive was toxic. Silence would settle in for the passengers.

This was never more apparent than the time he was driving me to the hospital for surgery and was on a conference call the entire time of the drive. I would have loved for him to ask me how I was feeling and for him to let me know that everything would be okay. But, it did not happen and I never told him how much that hurt me. What was I to do? I had said all I could say, did all I could do and it was never enough. I wanted his attention and to know that I mattered. I was the little girl all over again wanting the attention from her father. Here I am, forty plus years later wanting the attention from my husband. I was doing the same dance all over again. As a child I thought that I needed to perform for my father by being an honor student and here I am in my marriage doing things to get my husband to notice me. I was always on to the next thing; it was as if I always had to prove myself.

FINAL THOUGHTS

In every experience there is an opportunity to learn. It may take a minute, a day, or a lifetime, but to get it, is the biggest gift that can be given; to realize that all the hurt has been for my development and my growth into becoming a better me. I have come to the conclusion that I deserve better. I am the one that had to decide this, no one else could.

CHAPTER 6

WANTING TO BE WANTED

It's my belief that the desire to be wanted comes from our upbringing and how we were nurtured by our parents or the adults in our lives. If that emotional connection is not met or withheld for whatever reason, it leads to a life of longing to be wanted, loved, valued, understood, accepted, and appreciated. My parents did not meet this need for me; there is no blame because I know they did the best that they could with what they had. Their parents did not have the emotional tools to create a nurturing and loving environment for them as children and so the cycle continues. My parents loved me, but the words were seldom spoken and the warmth and security that you get from that feeling of being wanted, I never experienced.

I was tapped into the Honor Society in middle school and it was something for parents and family to attend. As we all stood on stage, with our special pins and certificates in hand, I looked out into the audience to see if anyone was there from my family and there was not. My mom was at work and she was not able to attend. To this day, I remember the feeling of disappointment and feeling alone.

Another time that I had this feeling is when my father would praise me after he had been drinking and that was about the only time he showed what seemed to be real affection. He would always brag about the fact that I made good grades and was on the honor roll. I felt uncomfortable because he did not do that with my brothers or sister and I did not like that kind of attention. Similarly, there were times that my second husband would not compliment an
achievement that I would make. I would assume it didn't matter to him or he had forgotten, when in fact

he would say it to other people, if it was something he could use to his benefit in conversation to make a connection with someone, he would pull the wife card with something that I had accomplished.
I always looked for the next opportunity to prove myself or to get his attention and it was not until I started to put my thoughts down on paper for this book, that I realized my entire second marriage was filled with moments of wanting to be wanted, or I should say "waiting to be wanted." I felt like I was left out. I was put through many awkward situations during the marriage where I was the last to know; the joke was on me. The neighbor walking over to get the keys to my Mercedes that had been sold was just one! Many times he would be sharing his upcoming purchases that were actually already purchased items, most of the time, or an upcoming trip that he would be going on or putting together that did not include me. To hear the information second hand or by overhearing others talk was humiliating as a spouse, it made me feel disrespected as a wife. I would say things at times, but most often I said nothing. I was treated like I was nothing; it was as if I didn't matter. I felt like nothing and when something was said it would be justified to pieces on his end, which only validated my feelings.

I was so checked out or numb in my first marriage that I didn't notice the feeling of my need to be wanted. While working days and my husband working nights, it wasn't something that I thought about often. It was more of me not being invested in the marriage and the overwhelming feeling of a means to get out of the childhood family home. I wanted to play, set up house, and do all of the things young married couples do.

The problem was we never connected on any kind of emotional level. My first husband was all about himself and much of his off time was spent with my father, fishing and drinking. So I was not on the priority list and again I fell silent and held my feelings. At this point, I had no idea who I was. The 10-year marriage did not end on a good note. I knew I did not want to stay in the marriage. We had a beautiful son together who never got to experience the beauty of a father and son relationship. His dad sadly enough was not present most of the time, so I took up as the only role model for our son. I have no regrets at all for that time in my life because it gave me an amazing boy who has grown into one of the most loving and compassionate men I will ever know.

I ended my first marriage without taking any time to figure out who I was as a woman and how I had ended up in this predicament. It is because of this I attracted a man that looked to have all the character traits that I craved from my first husband. In the beginning, this was someone with whom I shared amazing chemistry, love, and compassion. There was no denying our love for each other. I loved this man and wanted to spend the rest of my life with him.

I overlooked anything that could have been a red flag or a reason to hit the pause button on the relationship; I couldn't, it all felt so right. After a 10 year marriage that had no chemistry, this new found love, in my eyes, was all that I was looking for; it was a blessing. I knew he had a horrible temper, especially if things did not go his way. Yes, I knew he had ego that sometimes needed to be checked at the door. But, even with all of that, I skipped right over it until I couldn't any longer. Over time, the brunt of his anger would sometimes turn to the children or me and was usually delivered in a humiliating tone.

The company had become so successful and many of the employees would keep him on his pedestal that fueled his need to feel special and this for him was his own high. I longed for the days of that man who I knew could be vulnerable and compassionate, but they were few and far in between. Everyone acted on automatic, learning how to keep peace in the family and not irritate dad.

About 4 years ago, I decided I wanted to take charge of our anniversary trip and to make it a complete surprise for my husband. After many months of marriage counseling sessions, with the repeated complaints, I was told that I never took any initiative or wasn't spontaneous enough; I wanted to show my husband that I wanted to be the woman he desired and that I wanted to work on our relationship, I thought that I was doing just that.

I had planned, what I thought, would be the most amazing trip, to Santé Fe in an exclusive five-star boutique style hotel, with unbelievable rooms and each one being uniquely different. I set up cooking classes and dinners.You name it, I thought of it! I invested my heart and soul into making this trip a memorable experience. My husband and I agreed on a date and within a couple of months I needed to reschedule the date due to conflicts on my end. We agreed on another date and I recreated the same itinerary as the original date. We were maybe a month or so out and I brought up the trip and my husband told me that he didn't have it on his calendar, therefore he did not remember me giving it to him and that he could not go. I was so crushed, there was no offer of trying to figure out scheduling, it was more of something like, I had changed the dates so much that it took all of the excitement out of the surprise. The only thing I heard in my mind was, "I do not care enough about this marriage or you to make this happen." It was yet another confirmation that my husband was not interested in participating in our relationship.

FINAL THOUGHTS

As a child I wanted the approval of my parents, it's what I believe all children want. They wish to know that they matter in their parents eyes. I didn't have this from my parents. I then put this responsibility into my second husband's hands. I wanted to matter in his eyes. I tried everything and nothing worked. I had nothing left to say, nothing left to do. The very last thing I had was me. I was so busy trying to get him to do for me what I wasn't willing to do for myself. And that was to simply love and accept myself.

CHAPTER 7

GROWING APART

I loved my second husband unconditionally. I wanted to have his children and grow old with him. I wanted to be his partner, lover, and best friend for life. This is what I thought marriage was; mutual love, support, and respect for each other, until death do us part. The question then becomes, how is it possible to grow apart? What I now know is that in order to grow apart, you must first be together. It is not that we were complete strangers, but there was no feeling of being part of a team. My definition of a team is a united front, two people working together towards a common goal. You can't win a sport of any kind without precise communication and support of all of the players. I never felt that connection in our marriage. I allowed myself to be the silent partner and him to be the only player on the team.

My husband lived his life like a single man, sometimes with no regard for others' feelings. There were trips to Vegas, cruises, and all that comes with the life of a man with means. He had the freedom to do whatever he wanted. The more money we made, the more he did. There was always some new thing on order, or in the driveway. Boats, cars, motorcycles, jet skis, you name it, we had it. The latest and greatest! Most, if not all these purchases were made without my consent. He didn't feel the need to tell me, which made me feel insignificant as his wife. My opinion didn't appear to matter, meaning there was no sit down discussions about large purchases or our financial affairs. He would tell me, or not, after the fact, when in reality the decision was made and sharing it with me was an afterthought.

I mentioned this in a prior chapter, but it fits here nicely as well! I had a beautiful Mercedes convertible as my second car. Granted, I did not drive it very often, but that did not change the fact that it was my car and on a nice day it was great to have the option to take the convertible! I was completely blindsided one afternoon when my neighbor walked over, rang the doorbell, and asked me for the keys. My car had been sold to her! Since I did not know of this transaction, I had to play it off, as if I were aware of my car being sold. It was laughed off and told many times in the way of a joke. Again, this should have been another red flag as to the big picture and the fact he had no interest in my feelings. I do not believe he gave a second thought as to how I would feel, or the humiliation that I would experience because of his actions. This is just one of many instances where we were never on the same page. My husband was about business or the next deal and I was about raising the children and keeping the family unified. I did not pay attention to the signs early on in the relationship. I didn't want to acknowledge my true feelings. To be perfectly honest, part of his taking control was attractive to me at first. He handled everything and I thought this is what the head of the household did and I loved that feeling of safety and being taken care of by him.

Unfortunately, control turned out to be secrets, dismissiveness, and disrespect toward me as his partner. It was all about the next distraction, what he could purchase, or who he could impress. I can see that all of this was his attempt to fill a void that can never be filled with things. I believe this was the reason why most things were short lived in his "toy world." He was very much a here and now person, always looking for the next thing to pique his interest. Our personal world began to revolve around his business world that he worked very hard to create and the day-to-day craziness of employees, projects on the books, and all of the problems that go with that. My husband loved the thrill of a difficult situation and the confrontations that would come with it. He was always right and at times had no filter on how he would talk to people, a complete disrespect to the recipient of his anger.

For me, confrontation was the last thing I wanted to have with anyone. I always wanted everything to go smoothly. My husband was aware of this and knew that he could win any argument. He would go to great lengths to do so, even when he was caught in the middle of a lie, he was an expert at turning the tables to benefit him. I allowed him to believe he was right even when I knew at times that he was wrong.

For the majority of our marriage, I was on the home front raising the children and managing the house. We had three children involved in extracurricular activities, plus a large home and my own projects, so something was always going on. I wanted to be a part of something and I wanted to matter. I ran my own stationery business for 10 years, creating wedding invitations and birth announcements. I love paper of all kinds and had fun doing this, but it could also be demanding depending on the time of year. No matter how hard I worked at making my business work, he thought of it as a hobby. I was not a contributor to the household income and my business was always explained as the "tax deduction." I was always the brunt of a joke when it came to my doing something other than being his wife, taking care of the house, and raising the children. At moments, I felt that this was how he saw me, even though we met in the corporate world.

Here I was again, seeking approval from the man in my life. I continued finding ways to make myself stand out to my husband. I was on auto pilot trying to save my marriage and I was willing to do almost anything to keep our family together. I had given my husband several opportunities to choose me and our family. He would come in and out of the home, back and forth for over a six month span. Each time I allowed it, I believed the promise of change and his desire to be with his family. After rereading my journals, it was painfully obvious that we both were in denial.

The hardest thing I had to do was to admit to myself that nothing was working, my marriage was over. It would still take another few years before I was courageous enough to take action. I didn't forget about it, the inevitable divorce, I just put it on the back burner in my mind. Much like my siblings and I growing up, we kept waiting for the other shoe to drop. My husband did and does work harder than any man I know, but he played equally as hard and those times seldom included me. The times that we did have family time were typically interrupted with his work or there would be something that wouldn't go the way it should have and all hell would break loose. This is my perception of different scenarios with my husband, but it doesn't take away from the good times we shared. This is partially the reason I stayed, I knew that there was a part of him that I adored and loved. My perception of our relationship does not make it right or wrong but it's what I believe happened, it is my side of the story.

I did love my husband as I understood love. I mentioned before in a previous chapter, "you can't give what you don't have," and this applies to me as well. It is painfully obvious that I didn't love myself and because of this I allowed myself to be treated as such. I know that love is unconditional and this means without conditions. I am learning this on a daily basis, I get to practice walking the walk, with my now ex-husband. I am willing to let him be what he feels he needs to be, no more private investigating for me. It's easy to love him unconditionally because I no longer have any expectations. No need of his approval, his time, or his attention. Believe it or not, I can't begin to explain how freeing this is, to not let someone control your emotions day in and day out. The key word is "let," I allowed it all to happen. I doubt he even knew the role he played most of the time.

FINAL THOUGHTS

For a divorced couple we are in a good place. There is an unspoken respect I now feel while in his presence and I have the same for him. I have thought to myself, "Where was this person in the marriage?". But, I also am a realist and when you no longer have those deep emotional ties or expectations, everything comes to the surface and is easier to communicate. I have been blessed with the feeling of self-approval, which is ironic because my approving of myself should be and is all that matters.

CHAPTER 8

PUTTING ON THE FACE

As I reflect on the title of this chapter, I see how my entire relationship was about putting on the face. I have come to realize, over the months of working on this book, that I put on a mask to keep everything neat and tidy looking from the outside and not acknowledging my deepest feelings on the inside. I knew when my husband and I first met that he had anger issues. I knew this because we worked in the same office, I would see him from time to time and had witnessed his outbursts on several occasions. But, because it was always in the workplace and because it was work related, I thought it was the nature of his business. His outbursts made me feel very uncomfortable, but I would carry on even though it was humiliating for me. I was also embarrassed for him. This was definitely someone who could not control his temper and had no problem causing a scene. It didn't matter who it was or where we were, if he felt crossed or wronged, everyone in close proximity would hear about it. I didn't find out about this until after we were dating, the public outbursts and so on. I would put on the face as if all was well. After all, I was very good at hiding my true feelings.

One episode greatly sticks out to me: As the holidays approached, my husband and I had decided to separate once again. We told our children earlier in the month of December that we would each be moving into different houses the day after Christmas so that they would be prepared. We said something like "we are trying to find our way to figure ourselves out and our true feelings." The entire time we were telling each of them, I was thinking to myself "I KNOW MY WAY!" Before that, I thought my way was with him and with my family. I knew that this was about him trying to find out, again, what happiness is. I moved forward in my typical fashion, like so many times before, preparing to host a beautiful dinner party for our neighbors and friends. Acting as if all was well, pretending as if the emotional rug had not just been snatched from beneath my feet once more. It was a holiday tradition, which was something we always did as a couple. The evening for me was so horribly sad and yet my husband did not seem to be fased in the least bit. Our friends toasted us that evening, for the many fond memories shared between all of us over the years and wished us well. We were moving only a couple of miles away, but drastically downsizing in the effort of simplifying, or so we said. They did not know that this would most likely be the last of anything from us as a couple. My husband stood up and gave a gracious toast about the many good times we shared, on vacations and holiday weekends over the years with the other families in the neighborhood. All I could think was how detached he was as he talked, it all sounded so normal as I sat there like a Stepford wife, totally numb. He talked about the fond memories, while I could only remember the trips being miserable for the simple fact that I was always on high alert so as to not tick him off. There was no way I could show my true feelings about what was happening. I needed to "put on the face." By this time it was very natural and easy to wear the mask, this was truly devastating. I had mastered a lifetime of the disconnected look of shame and humiliation with empty smiles and apologies.

I have learned that this behavior stemmed from my need to put on a face for my family as a child. After watching how my brothers were treated and disrespected by my father, how could I look at my father with an honest face and let him see how much I disliked him for what he did to our family? How could I keep an honest face after such an experience? Although, I was disgusted by my father's behavior towards my brothers, I never had the courage to tell him. If I couldn't tell him the truth, then what's left? I had to put on the face and act as if nothing happened. I acted as if it didn't bother me because I never said otherwise. I shudder to think what would have happened if I had shown my resentment towards him for how he had treated them, as well as my mother. I believe my brothers' lives would have been different had our parents been more supportive and nurturing. I also believe my parents' lives would have been different had their parents been more nurturing, my father may have had more compassion for the boys. He had a preconceived idea as to what it meant to be a man, to be tough. If this were not so, then the boys could have had a different upbringing and we all would have had an opportunity to have a better childhood.

This is not to say once we become of age that we're not responsible for our lives. It is what happens before we're responsible adults that shapes us into young men and women. I believe that everyone should be given a healthy foundation, a springboard of stability that catapults us into a life of emotional balance. If not, we can choose to get counseling or we can just choose to forgive and let it all go. What I do know, without a doubt, is that both brothers, up until the day they both died, were looking for the approval of my father, especially my older brother. Again, I have never said one word to my father about his mistreatment of them. I can say that even in death, my brother doesn't have my father's approval. As a mother, I thought by shielding my children from the craziness and dysfunction meant that I was being a good mother. I hoped that they would not be affected. I was so wrong. I can see it has affected each of them in a different way. Fortunately, I have since learned that it is never too late to make a difference.

FINAL THOUGHTS

It is in this moment that I am willing to share my story, so they may have an opportunity to change their feelings about their childhood, no matter what they have experienced. It is my wish that they realize that the drama had nothing to do with them and is in no way a reflection on them as children and now as young adults. The truth of the matter is that my ex-husband and I had our own issues before marrying, that we needed to heal individually.

CHAPTER 9

WAITING FOR HIM TO CHANGE

I stayed for the promise of change. It was something that I wanted so badly and when I would hear the words "I want to change, I want my wife and family," it was enough for me to go on for another few years, when in reality his desire to change never really surfaced for any length of time. It would be 20 plus years before it hit me that nothing was going to change. That my husband was not interested in changing. As each promise was broken, a part of me would shut down.

My family and friends only saw me as living the "American Dream." The beautiful family, lavish homes, fancy cars, boats, and five star vacations. It was a beautifully wrapped package on the outside but on the inside I was empty. For me, these things began to mean nothing if we could not enjoy them together. Unfortunately, very few "toys" got used, as most would sit, once the honeymoon phase was over. As our income increased, so did the possessions. Don't get me wrong, I love nice things, but not when they come with a price. Everyone paid a price, for me it was not having my husband around because he was so busy building the business. We did have our moments of joy together, but they were few and far between. I know that our children missed out on their father not being home as often as they would have liked. So in place of being absent came the material things that would distract us all for a brief moment and once the thrill was gone we were back to the same issues. The long days turned into long empty nights as travel began to happen for out of town trade shows, entertaining clients, and exploring new areas to grow the business. I watched the person I thought I knew become someone I did not recognize anymore. There was very little time spent at home and when it was, we would do all of the social things couples do: dinners out, charity events, couples vacations, but it never seemed quite right to me; something was missing. I would hang out with my woman friends but rarely with the person I came with and who I really wanted to spend quality time with, my spouse. I began to question myself, was I no longer attractive, was my body repulsive, was I too boring? All of these things raced through my head at any given time. We had three children at home and I was involved in PTA, girl scouts, fundraisers, club sports, carpooling, vacation bible school; you name it, I had my hand up to volunteer. I was hopeful, or was it my being gullible. Whatever the case may be, I was in it for the duration, for hope and his promises of change. I loved my husband and I wanted nothing more than my family to be together. That is what I kept telling myself. Now, I know it was an idea in my head of what I wanted my marriage and family to be, that vision of unity, growing old together, reaping the rewards of our success together, and watching our children grow up and have their own families. All of these things still are happening but it will not be with their mom and dad as husband and wife. I see the good in everyone and I always saw the good in my husband; he was extremely intelligent and good looking with a quick sense of humor. I could no longer hold onto just the good in him, it was not enough to sustain me emotionally and certainly not enough to base a marriage on. I wanted to be the master multitasker. I wanted to be wanted and yes, I was exhausted, it all took its toll on my mental and physical health. Yet, I never said, "Hey, something is wrong with this picture!" I just kept questioning myself internally and doubting everything.

This went on for years and I became more and more disconnected as I continued acting on autopilot. I ran the household and made everything seem normal for those looking from the outside. After being confronted, my husband confessed to having a long-term affair. I have no words to describe the gut wrenching feeling that ripped through me and in that instant my life and my children's lives would forever be changed. Fear gripped me at the thought of losing my husband. What would I do alone? How could I raise my children without their father in the home? Who would ever want me? I have nothing to offer anyone. Everything I thought of was all fear based. Looking back now, oh my of course, I could be on my own and be content with just me! I was already alone, just living with another person, that at the end of the day gave me very little to hang on to. Yet, it would be years before I accepted the fact that he was not going to change and that I was the one that needed to take ownership of myself and stop waiting for him to show up in the marriage.

I gave him everything I thought he wanted, I was his biggest supporter. I was loving, kind, and compassionate! I thought that I was being a good wife by giving him his space, after all he did mention that he felt like he was living in a "fish bowl," which was said when he thought I was asking too many questions. I strived for a stress free household environment even though the greatest stress in the household was him and his volatile temper and mood swings. It was normal for everyone to be on guard and mindful of our P's and Q's as to not upset Dad.

Now as I reflect back, the very existence that I was trying to avoid is the exact life I lived. I didn't want to be rejected and for the most part I was ignored, looked over, and taken for granted, there was no consideration for my feelings, or anybody's for that matter.

Much like that of my childhood and watching how my father disrespected my mother over and over again, he was never home and when he was he was always preoccupied with something or in a bad mood. I don't ever remember my dad and us, as a family, just sitting around and watching TV; it just never happened.

FINAL THOUGHTS

I was waiting and praying for God to change my husband and heal our family, when in reality I needed to pray for the change in me. For the strength and courage to face the truth and to accept what he is unable to give; I am grateful to be in this place of awakening, with the opportunity to share in this beautiful way.

CHAPTER 10

FORCED TO FIND MY VOICE

Growing up in a household where my parents argued constantly shaped my perception about what I believed I could be, say, or do as a person. I can't remember a moment in my childhood where I was encouraged to share my feelings. I felt that I couldn't, or shouldn't, speak up. As the old saying goes, "A child should be seen and not heard," was the order of the day. As I grew up, a child talking back was looked at as being disrespectful. I wanted to allow my children to have a voice; I noticed that by covering up for my husband's anger issues and by making excuses invalidated my children's voices and feelings. Honestly, I did not realize that I didn't have a voice until I couldn't speak up about something that someone in my life had said or done. When I was bothered by something someone said, I didn't voice my feelings or opinion. I believe it was from watching my parents argue that I decided I didn't like confrontation and fighting. The thought of someone raising their voice was something I wasn't going to tolerate, however my life was filled with all of that and more. In my desire to avoid drama and run away from it, I landed in two marriages filled with the thing that I was running away from.

The idea of no confrontation would mean that I would have to stay quiet. I would allow the men in my life to twist my words, to turn the table and have me believe their bullshit. I developed a high tolerance for the lies. I became accustomed to allowing myself to be indirectly disrespected in my marriage. That's what I did on a regular basis until it made me emotionally and physically sick and even then I believed more of the B.S. because I wanted the idea of love; I wanted my husband to love me. Once I made a comment that my husband and I didn't argue, it was only because I was willing to keep quiet. I knew when to speak, I would wait until I was really pissed, then speak sideways and it was never directly about the issue. I would get little jabs in when I could. I remember hearing someone say, "when you are arguing about the light switch, it is usually not about the light switch." At the right opportunity, I allowed my withheld anger to seep out as harsh comments.

We would then get into an argument which I thought was making a difference, but boy was I wrong. My husband drained the energy out of me, with his fast double talking, until I would give up and leave the conversation. I was tired of the back and forth. I realized I wanted to keep quiet because I wanted my marriage to work. I allowed my husband to be right, even when I knew what he had done or said was completely wrong. Those moments of conceding may have settled the house, but it did nothing for my mind, body, and soul. I slowly started to lose my grip on what I thought was reality, everything started to slowly fall apart. I couldn't keep up the pretense. I couldn't pretend that it was okay for him to ignore me and treat me like an outsider. I was desperate to keep up the façade but I had lost my way. I prayed for him to change, I believed in him and the goodness that I saw from time to time throughout our marriage.

I have since realized that the person that needed to change was me, and so I did. I had accumulated so much hurt and resentment for how I had allowed myself to be treated. I knew something needed to change. I kept making excuses for my husband and for my tolerating his lack of respect for me and our marriage. There were plenty of opportunities for me to speak up, but again I never did. I overlooked his behavior, for the sake of my family and all that we had built together. I told myself we could always go to marriage counseling and was excited that my husband agreed to partake in the potential healing of our marriage. I now know that both parties must want the relationship to work, it must be what they want to do as a couple. One can't go to counseling to try to appease the other, it must be an understanding between the two that a common goal is the purpose or it will never work. I believe that the only reason my husband participated in those sessions was to get me off his back. He wanted me to believe that he was trying to work on our marriage. His heart was never in it, I was only prolonging the inevitable.

Therapy is for the individual, not the marriage. It must be addressed in a way that each person is willing to take responsibility for their own happiness. I can now see that I was looking to my husband for my happiness, while he was seeking what he believed made him happy. Truth be told, most of the time it didn't include me. This is not to say that there were not moments of joy, but the opposite was front and center 65% of our marriage.

My husband would sometimes pull interesting stunts I thought to be funny and at times it was. He wouldn't think twice about embarrassing you, but if the table was turned he would lose it! It was my birthday and my husband and I were out with six other couples. We had plans for a wonderful dinner and a concert to follow. My husband thought it would be funny to push my face into the cake. I got extremely upset and called him out. I was pissed and asked him, "How would you feel if I were to do that to you? You wouldn't like it one bit, would you?" He was embarrassed that I called him out on his behavior and because of it he left and did not return for the entire evening.

I remember another interesting experience: My husband and I had taken a trip to Atlantic City with two other couples. I thought this would be the perfect time to reconnect with my husband. I had given him a letter that I had poured my love and soul into. In short, I said that I was grateful for this time to get reacquainted with each other. He was mad at the fact that I had given him this letter and accused me of ruining his trip. He then avoided me the entire time. I had to act as if it didn't bother me, again! I had never felt so alone, it was a horrible experience. As I write these words, I see the pattern unfolding before my eyes. I see the little girl wanting to be wanted, to be noticed and appreciated. I spent most of my marriage wanting to be wanted. I wanted my husband to love me just for being his wife and the mother of his children. I did all I could to be the woman or wife he wanted and needed. I can honestly say that I don't think he knows what he needs in a woman.

FINAL THOUGHTS

It is from our experiences that we discover the person that we are capable of being. I must say that I've learned a lot about myself because of the men I chose to marry. I could not tell these stories if it were not for them. I would not be the woman that I am today, if it were not for all that has shaped me into the person that I am, one that is willing to learn from her life experiences no matter how challenging they may be. More importantly, I am willing to share my truth so that someone else may learn from my choices, with the hope they may become the person they are meant to be.

CHAPTER 11

LIES WE TELL OURSELVES

I am an honest person, almost to a fault, or so I thought! I have always been a rule follower and I guess it goes back to not wanting to get into trouble as a child. I would always do the right thing, over and over again.

But if I'm to be completely honest with myself, the lies we tell ourselves in our head to make everything seem ok, are the lies that I'm talking about now. Better yet, withholding the truth about how we really feel to keep from being confrontational or hurting someone's feelings. So, we tell our family and friends what they want to hear. I am not talking about being disrespectful or rude to someone, but the truth of how you feel about a situation or behavior that does not sit well with you.

In my life, I had surrounded myself with people that had no problem lying to my face; I knew it and I said nothing. It would take a lot for me to reach my breaking point, so I found myself allowing people to disrespect me on so many levels. I never considered that I was the one holding my own lie by not speaking my truth and by enabling them to continue to lie whenever it served them. I made it easy to be treated this way and made all kinds of excuses for their behavior in my head by tucking it under the rug and going on like nothing had happened.

I allowed myself to be manipulated, for the sake of my relationships, it didn't matter the person, it could have been with my spouse, a friend, or family members. I thought of it as a way of keeping or "hanging on to the relationship." It was my way of not having to deal with any drama or the issue at hand; I was just going with the flow. Taking the high road, when in fact all I was doing was carrying the emotional burden for the sake of what I thought was a true relationship.

The reality was I became a doormat disguised as the easygoing, fun-loving person, that never let things get to her. The entertainer, the hostess, the quirky mom, and wife all wrapped into one!

The behavior came naturally to me because as I moved through my childhood, I tried to save my brothers from an emotionally and physically abusive father and would carry that burden on my shoulders to try to make everything okay. I wanted to shield them from the pain. I remember feeling embarrassed for my brothers and I would get that gut wrenching feeling in the pit of my stomach when my father would belittle them with his harsh words.

I never stood up to my father, ever! I never voiced my opinion about how wrong that was and how he had taken away my brother's' innocence, their self-esteem, and their feeling of safety and replaced it with fear and instability. There were times of joy in our household but we all lived waiting for the other shoe to drop. I personally believe my parents did not have respect for themselves, so how could they respect us as children? It became very uncomfortable for me to not say anything, it made me feel ashamed and guilty because by not speaking the truth meant that I condoned or allowed the behavior. In my father's case, why would he do anything different? Nobody, including myself, stood up to him and told him how they felt.

I carried this all of my life, up until the point of owning the reality of the person that I was capable of being. That is when my journey to self-discovery and healing began. I learned to love myself for me and me only. I slowly saw myself change and become stronger, healthier, and no longer fearful of the future. "What you permit, you promote," is a quote that could have been my lifelong tagline and how true it resonated with me. That is how I lived most of my life. I thought I was keeping the peace, when actually I was teaching people how to treat me. By not speaking up, it meant that whatever was or had been done or said was fine with me, especially with my husband. The truth for me was, I allowed my relationship to be fueled by fear and insecurity, along with my unwillingness to speak up for myself. I let many things go unsaid, that I did not agree with or believe, but that is where the lying to self comes in. I thought it made me the bigger person even when I knew something was wrong. I started to resent my husband for me having to dance around my words with him, so that they did not seem accusatory or appear as if I was questioning him, because if so, he would get angry and that would be a whole different dance.

This recurring behavior gave me the courage that I needed to get real and face the truth. In the past, I was willing to give him other chances because I wanted nothing more than our marriage. When you have shared most of your life with someone and created memories, built a thriving business, lived in your dream home and had it all, it is hard to let that history go, even more so when you have children. But, there is no marriage if only one person is interested in participating and that became the hard truth. That was my final push; I was ready to validate all of those gut feelings that I had been able to keep at bay for so many years.

The thing that brought us together was no longer enough to keep us together and that was one of the hardest things for me. I learned a lot from my marriage and would not trade the last 26 years for anything. In spite of all of our flaws, we had some amazing times as a couple, and as a family, and for that I am grateful. The man that I fell madly in love with and who I know without question loved me, to this day has many beautiful qualities. We are a blend of two parents, three amazing children, and two grandchildren that will always keep us as a family, not like we were, but a redefined family unit that has taken on a different feel and is still filled with unconditional love.

FINAL THOUGHTS

My hopes and dreams were for a marriage that would last until the end of our lives, a marriage filled with love, affection, respect for one another, and oh so much fun! The idea of the perfect marriage and what it could have been if we both worked on and invested in our marriage was my biggest feeling of loss. It is now my time to redefine what love means to me, so I can give this to myself first and then to the world, unconditionally.

CHAPTER 12

EMOTIONAL SCARS

What are emotional scars? When we think of a scar, we think of it as something visible on the outside of one's body. An emotional scar buries itself deep into your core and many times no one on the outside knows it is there. Emotional scars occur in different ways, such as being intentionally belittled by degrading words and or behaviors, or anything that makes a person feel less than and not valued.

In my case, I did not see myself as having emotional scars, I just knew I wanted to get out of my parents' house, leave behind the crazy environment and get away from my controlling father. Everything that we hear about children being like sponges and picking up on all the characters traits of the people in their surroundings is true. I had no idea that my parents' behavior and the things that I lived, watched, and heard growing up, would shape my life and the person that I would become as a wife and mother. My parents arguing on a regular basis made the perfect impression on me as to what I thought a relationship looks like. I had nothing else to compare it to. What I garnered from that is that I wanted to be loved, to feel wanted, and valued.

It killed me inside to witness the physical abuse my brother's endured. I watched part of them being stripped away with every episode. I know that this greatly affected their self-esteem and self-worth. My oldest brother was a competitive boxer and was in amazing physical shape. There was a time where he could have stood up to my father and caused bodily damage, but he never did; he would always back down. My younger brother would have never stood up to my father and you could see the impact it had on both of them as they each lived very reckless lives and abused alcohol, just as my father did. All they ever wanted was my father's approval and to feel loved and wanted. Unfortunately, it was something that my father was never able to give them in their lifetime.

My youngest brother died at the age of 28 and more recently my oldest brother at the age of 60. Even as a grown man, my oldest brother was still searching for approval from my dad, but it never came, not even after his death. I spent years trying to make everything okay for my brothers. They always had money or legal struggles and unfortunately did not take ownership of their own lives. My now ex-husband and I were always rescuing them in so many ways. It is my hope that this book in some way validates their lives and how courageous they both were for enduring what they did, as children and as men. They both had so many beautiful qualities about them and the most genuine hearts and souls. I will not pretend that I have the answers for why my father did what he did, but what I did notice is that he had parents just as disconnected as he was and I could see where he could have gotten emotionally side tracked.

As for my mother, she was not abusive like my dad, but she tolerated his behavior for years and would stay busy at church or in the school system. The point is when we are not willing to really take a look at ourselves and be honest about our behaviors, we look for ways to distract ourselves.

For my father, it was drinking and numbing the pain that he could never admit or express. It never worked, it only created an angry man who caused such destruction to his family and sometimes those around him. I do understand now how all the dysfunction starts or never ends, it just falls into place from one generation to the next. Everyone automatically does what was done to them under the excuse of "it is how I was raised or how my father and mother treated me." If the time is not taken to examine yourself and your feelings, you will always distract yourself with other addictions and behaviors. It is when you see who you are and acknowledge what you are becoming, or have become, that you should want to change the cycle. Which is easier said than done.

What I did know was that I was going to be different when it came to my children. I wanted them to be able to have a voice, to know that they were loved and valued by my words and my actions. I did not feel that as a child growing up, even though I knew that my parents loved me. How could they give me what they did not have to give? If I am to consider my parent's behavior, then I must take into consideration my own relationship with my husbands or lack thereof. I now believe it was the "unhealed aspects" of my husband's past that were visibly present on a daily basis, in both my marriages. They had never taken the time to redefine themselves or their past. So what I ended up with in both marriages, was the same thing I was running from, dysfunction, anger, chaos, and emotional abuse.

I was totally unaware that my growing up in a household with all the makings of (the Jerry Springer Show) would be the foundation of what I would take into marriage. As a child, I was invisible; as a wife, I shifted into the same role. I did not like confrontation of any kind, if I questioned my husband about something that he did not want to answer, it would easily be twisted back to something about me. His words were cutting and his tone was harsh. I would usually smooth the conversation over with meaningless words and stuff it all inside like it never took place. That became our pattern in the later years of marriage and I still had not found my voice.

Before writing this book, I could see the connection. Not once did I think that I was like my mother. I watched her being mistreated by my father over and over again. She was a firecracker and could hold her own, but she paid a price for allowing herself to do the dance each time. It never crossed my mind that they should get a divorce, it's just the way it was. The fights could be explosive one minute and the next minute, all was calm like nothing happened.

I see the cycle unfolding before my eyes. My children have said to me that they have felt invisible at times, which was the exact thing that I experienced throughout my childhood. I see that I am like my mother and my husband's character traits were that of my father: insecurities and lack of emotional control. I see there is no difference at all, the explosive temper, cursing, and disrespect, it is all the same. Unbeknownst to me, I had lived out the exact relationship that my parents had.

FINAL THOUGHTS

But by the grace of God, I am here to share my story. I am feeling free and inspired to live a new dream. Life has taught me a valuable lesson. Through this journey, I have awakened to new levels.

CHAPTER 13

FINDING VALUE IN SELF

In the midst of my life, I was on automatic and on a road to nowhere. I was depleted of all emotion; my willingness to do what was right for me at the time was wishful thinking. I had nothing more to give. I had plenty of years of experience of being disconnected, as I watched my mother and father in a marriage that was filled with drama. I had often wondered how she could have stayed in a volatile relationship. Who knew some years later, that I would get the answer to my question through my own firsthand experience. I was so busy in the turmoil that I didn't have time to think or reflect. I don't think I knew what those words even meant. By the time of my second marriage, I was very disconnected from any sense of self. I wasn't interested in me; I wanted to be whatever I needed to be for my husband. This had now become my number one goal, along with taking care of my children.

In my childhood, the emotional and physical abuse became the norm. It was something that we just accepted. I never accepted it but because I was a little girl and had no power I just tucked it away within me, pretending that all was well. I threw myself into my studies, in hopes of being a good girl.

As a child there wasn't much that I could do and I knew that I wanted out of that life the moment that I was old enough to leave and I did! Actually, it was partly the reason for marrying my first husband. I wanted to get away from my drama filled life. By this time I had a full young life filled with fighting and arguing and unknowingly, it had become my norm. I was unaware that I had become immune to angry and mean spirited people and more tolerable of disrespect and mistreatment. Somewhere inside me I believed that it was okay. I saw my mother hanging in there, taking the B.S. from my father on a regular basis and for me it was the very character traits that I emulated throughout my life. I was hanging in there trying to make it work, while taking all the mistreatment and disrespect that they could dish out towards me. I say this because for many years I would make excuses for such behavior. I think it was less painful if I could justify it. I would say to the kids, "Dad has been working really hard and is stressed out. Don't take his tantrum or anger personally, he loves you."

It has been a long journey to finding my value. I had tolerated the discomfort of a dysfunctional childhood, it was what I saw on a regular basis. I had no other experience to draw from. There was nothing to do, nor did I have the proper tools to process the emotional and sometimes traumatizing abuse. I thought by leaving my house that my troubles would be over, but nothing could have been further from the truth. I was helpless and just wanted it to be over; to grow up and move out. It's not to say that most people do not have some form of dysfunction that they must overcome, but this was mine.

I feel my story is important because when we are willing to tell the truth, we see that we are not alone. I know that someone will see themselves in my story and be inspired to do something about it, hopefully sooner than later. I also wish to break the cycle of dysfunction in my family, in this lifetime. I wish to live a life of true happiness, which is starting now! I pray this inspires my daughters to new levels of possibilities and opportunities, to discover their power as young women. As I am willing to value myself, I am also willing to lead the way to a new way of being.

In finding value in myself, I no longer want to make excuses for inappropriate behavior or disrespectful people, especially for the people in my immediate circle and immediate family. I have tried to stay clear of any scenario that reflects the one I lived for most of my adult life. I know the challenges and lies that one must tell themselves to stay and I have no judgment. Those that thought that I should leave my marriage could not have dragged me away from my husband. It had to be my decision; I couldn't leave until I was truly ready. I hope these individuals come to their own conclusion and discover something better. When that moment comes, I will be there to offer my support.

I now see that we connect with people that we feel will make our lives better. Sometimes they do and other times they give us the opportunity to grow. In this particular relationship, I was willing to forget myself. I knew it was a lie; I was lying to myself. More importantly, I knew he was lying to me. If I am not honest with myself, then how is it possible for someone to be honest with me? Will I recognize it if they were? We see what we want to see, even if we have reservations. We want what we want and will tell ourselves what we need to, to make it okay for us to have what we feel we so desperately need. I recently read a profound statement by Brene Brown: "The most powerful stories are the ones we tell ourselves, but beware they're usually fiction." How true that is! I can remember the things I would tell myself to justify his behavior.

In the beginning, I believed my husband because I trusted him and as time went on the trust had been broken. I wanted more than anything to believe what I was hearing, but in the end, after the trust continued to be broken, it was like looking at someone I didn't know at all. I wanted to believe him and I wanted to make him my world. I depended on him for my happiness. It was made clear to him how much I loved him. I thought that I was clear about his love for me. Looking back, how could I be clear about anything? I entered this relationship with the same emotional baggage that I had left home with, nothing was really unpacked or processed. I was too busy trying to be what I thought he needed. I had become an expert at being what I needed to be, for him and everyone else who needed me. I knew that I had reached a turning point when I could no longer believe the lies. I had endured all that I could and I allowed my children to witness me pretending that it was okay, allowing myself to be disrespected. I made more excuses than I care to mention. I thought I was doing well by them, but it did not turn out the way that I thought it would. My children were also not immune to the lies and my playing along did not shield them from embarrassment and pain.

FINAL THOUGHTS

It was a long time coming and as I started to get stronger the need to prove the lies became unimportant because I knew in my gut what was truth and what was not. This was the moment I knew it was over. I could no longer see my husband and our relationship in the same way. I no longer saw myself in the same way. In this moment, I knew that this life that I had come to know was over and I took my first step in the right direction, my first step to value myself!

CHAPTER 14

WHAT ABOUT THE CHILDREN

I believe that children are the lost victims of a chaotic or dysfunctional household. When there is so much going on within and around the family unit, who has time to honestly consider the children's feelings? We tend to assume they are caught up in their own stuff or distracted by their friends and playdates, but the reality is that children don't miss anything. They may not know the full details, but they pick up quickly that mom is distracted and seems sad or dad is away all of the time or is quick to anger.

I always tried to buffer my children from pain, hurt, and sadness in all areas of their lives. I wanted everything to be happy and light all of the time. If I could not fix it with cupcakes, then it would be a shopping trip or anything to take their minds off of hurt or disappointment. As my children grew older, if their dad did something or said something hurtful, I would console them and would create excuses for his behavior. When they would ask, "Why is dad gone so much?" I would go over with them how busy he is and why he needed to be gone all the time. I said it was to keep things going for the business, in turn keeping us in the style of living we had all grown accustomed to. If it were a guy's trip it would sound like, "Your dad works hard and deserves some R&R." Just distract with excuses for him, so they don't have to feel! How very wrong I was, by taking those feelings away from them, even though it came from a place of love, I was not helping them. When my children became teenagers it hit home that they deserved the truth and not a sugar coated excuse or cupcake to make everything go away. When I refer to the truth it does not have to be blunt facts, but enough for them to begin to process the situation at their level.

I often wondered about my mother and how she could have stayed. I hate the word abuse, but that is what happened in my childhood home, at some level it was on a daily basis. Whether it was verbal or physical makes no difference to the recipient, the pain is all the same. The answer became very clear, "I am my mother!" I allowed chaos in my home by not standing up for myself and by not using my voice and my children paid the price. I allowed myself to be disrespected over and over again. Boundaries were crossed and ignored over and over again. My children watched the dance repeat itself the last several years of my marriage. I was so disconnected and too frozen to make a move. I stayed for what I called love and for the sake of the family. I was no different than my mother back in the day! Although I would get upset, there were times that I did not stand up for the children when it came to their father's temper. I would patch up the holes with words, a hug, and go ahead with the family dinner as planned, exactly as my mother did after a horrible argument with my father.

I was preoccupied with the vision of what a family looks like and how to make everyone happy and just be okay. By that I mean I loved the family traditions, the special meals that I would do for even the smallest of the holidays, the little things like on Valentine's Day decorating the table with beautiful dinnerware, flowers, and cooking a great meal which included giving little gifts to the family. The amazing vacations that I would spend months planning all in the name of family. I was always planning the next "fun" thing we all could do but the truth of it all is that the holidays, the elaborate vacations, things that families do together, all came with some kind of a price. I can't remember one vacation that there was not an outburst or tantrum from my husband, if something went wrong or broke, he would be quick to anger and everyone would just get quiet and let him run his course; any kind of a protest or to question him would only make him more mad. At times we all walked on eggshells just because it was easier that way, much like myself as a little girl never to bring attention to myself. In time, I could no longer shield my children and make everything okay or come up with rose-colored excuses. They figured it out for themselves and words weren't necessary.

My life has been a byproduct of a childhood without the emotional stability and support of my parents. There is no blame here, it is important to know that I am shedding light on a life lived disconnected from self. In thinking about this chapter, I thought it was important to get each of my children's thoughts on their childhood and family life growing up. They shared their truth as they remembered it, they were each different, yet uniquely the same. They too had feelings of being invisible and not having a voice at times. Although nothing was too devastating, it opened my eyes to things that I simply was numb to knowing. So here was the most beautiful opportunity to do it differently.

I sat with each of my children and apologized for not being a more present parent in their lives when it came to listening, validating them, and standing up for them. For not using my voice when it was called for and most importantly not letting them use their voice. It sounds so simple, yet was extremely powerful for them to hear from me, as it would have been for me as a child or even as an adult from my parents.

What I wanted and needed from my parents was to know that I mattered and was truly loved! I know that they love me, but honestly warm hugs and the words "I love you" have never been given freely. So I get to do it differently with my children. Moving forward I am making an honest effort to be all that I can be by living in the present and not looking outside of myself for love and support from anyone. The men in my life did not love themselves, so how could they love me? There was nothing for them to give me emotionally.

My parents came together with emotional scars from their childhood and they looked to each other to fill that void and make each other happy in the name of love. In all the years of their marriage, that void has never come to be filled and the fighting has not stopped. If anything, I hear my mother say things to my dad that tells me there is still so much unresolved pain. It became clear to me once I looked at my life and the men that I have loved, and I can now see the truth. We were just like my parents coming together with our unhealed selves. Getting married, having a family, and playing house; add the pressures of life and eventually the truth must surface and it did. Do we acknowledge this or do we pretend all is well and keep moving forward like most do, like I did. I stayed until I had nothing more to give, no more faces, no more fronts, no more pretending being put to the side did not bother me. The time was now to break the cycle. My children needed to see their mother take ownership of her life and no longer be invisible. My daughters needed to see that marriage is equal on both sides and that they should be cherished and feel wanted and valued. If they were to never see me make such a life change, then guess what, they would be living their lives in the same cycle of denial and for my son the same in many ways. I have even more regrets when it comes to him. He has had two fathers, that have set examples for him, and while he has learned much in the way of worldly things, there is so much more that fathers give to their sons that he was not given. In spite of that, he is one of the most loving, gentle, and patient fathers to his young sons that I have ever seen. It is a beautiful thing to watch how he interacts with them.

FINAL THOUGHTS

I love my three children, and above all else, I know that my ex-husband does too. His love for them has never been in question. It all comes down to these words, "We teach people how to treat us." I now live by these words and remind my children all the time of the importance of being the person they want to be and to be true to themselves.

CHAPTER 15

FORGIVENESS

In order to make sense of my life, I needed to ask myself two important questions: "What does it mean to forgive?" and "What does forgiveness mean?" The definition of forgiveness is "an intentional and voluntary process by which a victim undergoes a change in feeling and attitude regarding an offense, let's go of negative emotions such as vengefulness, with an increased ability to wish the offender well." Oprah's definition is "giving up the hope that the past could be any different, letting go so the past does not hold you prisoner and not holding onto grudges and anger." What I have come to know is that forgiveness is a process and as much as we would like it, it does not happen overnight. I can say that all day long, but how I really feel will be seen in my behavior and in my words. If I haven't done the work then there will be a level of discomfort somewhere in my body. I may ignore it, but it's there and if we ignore the pent-up energy, it will find a way to express itself. In my opinion, this energy then turns on you in the way of disease and sickness. I did not really understand the meaning of forgiveness and that followed me throughout my life, asserting itself in all of my affairs for the opportunity to be released. I thought I could ignore the hurt and shame that I experienced as a child and not look at it ever again. When looking at my environment, it was obvious why I would have issues with processing my feelings and ignoring them. Back then I thought that if you wanted to survive you kept to yourself and did what you were told.

I harbored my true feelings: of insecurity, fear, and self-doubt; these feelings haunted me for most of my adult life. I would attract people into my world that would reflect back to me these emotions. What else could I harvest with these feelings but more of the same? I see that now, but back then I thought that I was free from all the drama. At the time, I didn't know that forgiveness is an experience, that it is more than words and just saying, "I forgive you," isn't enough. It's about processing the feeling associated with the unhealed issue. In order to process the feeling I needed outside help, more than just from family and friends.

I sought out the help of a therapist and with her help I was able to break down so many things that I never stopped to look at because it was too uncomfortable. As I've mentioned previously, I have never said anything to my parents about their behavior and the affect it had on us as children. It is much more than that because my brothers' lives were shaped by that experience up until the very end. My sister and I have the opportunity to make a difference in our lives by being honest with our parents and stop pretending that it didn't exist. In talking with my sister as I started to put this book together, I see that her feelings closely resembled mine and oddly enough I have found comfort in that. I thought that because it was over and the fact that my parents are much older, what could it really do to bring all of this up now? Do I want my parents to experience unnecessary pain at this point in their lives? How can I forgive someone if they don't know what I'm forgiving them for? If my parents are unaware of the effect our upbringing has had on us, then is it necessary for me to bring it up to them? Will I ever truly be released from my past if healing does not take place? Although I did feel responsible for my brothers' well-being, I never said anything. So the question remains the same. How can I forgive them if I haven't told them my truth? This is the perfect example of my believing that it is more important for me to avoid hurting someone no matter how wrong their behavior may have been. This was me avoiding a potential confrontation. In the moment it may feel better to not say anything, but not letting it go has proven to have long lasting effects on any and every one in close proximity of their dysfunction.

I could not be the woman that I've become if I was not honest with them, more importantly I have to be honest with myself. I don't have to pretend anymore. I no longer have to make excuses for bad behavior. I did this for most of my marriage and now that I know better, I can't pretend that I don't know what I know! It's also important to forgive myself, for not speaking up for my siblings, on occasions for not speaking up for my children, and most of all for the many times, too many times to count, of not standing up for me. This is where it must start, I must forgive myself first for not being stronger, for not being whatever I thought I needed and tried to be, and everything else. If I had stood up for myself I would be telling a different story. There were times that I did stand up for myself in my marriage, but I can see that it is not really standing up for me if I allow the behavior to continue. My now ex-husband and I have had conversations in the past in which he has apologized for his actions in our marriage and for the way he treated me. For me not to accept that from him and to keep bringing up the past, serves no one. I do wish that the past could have been different but the reality is, it was not. So for the sake of myself and for my children, I choose forgiveness and only wish to move forward, in a new defined relationship.

Although I could talk about this for days, the fact still remains the same: I must forgive myself first and then it is easy to forgive others. I see the importance of telling my truth. It is not about my parents, it has always been about me; discovering that I deserve to be treated with respect. Discovering that I matter just the way I am. In order for me to live the life that I imagine, there can be no unhealed emotions lingering from my past. I am willing to look at the truth and release it once and for all, as I have stated before, it all starts with me.

FINAL THOUGHTS

I am sharing my story with my parents to give myself the emotional freedom to love completely. It has never been to hurt them; this has never been my intention, at all. It has been to release the burden of shame and guilt that I've carried around for most of my life. I can only speak from a loving place and hope that they listen with an open heart. I am not expecting anything in return; forgiveness is the gift that I am giving to myself. It is also for the sake of my brothers and their emotional freedom.

CHAPTER 16

LIFE AFTER DIVORCE

When I began to prepare for this book, I was only thinking about myself and the possible benefits of healing that closure would bring. I had to be willing to let go of the past, not to forget it, but to redefine what it meant to be me. To redefine myself and what it meant to be a single and on my own. The fear of this new life was terrifying, not to mention the thought of being out in the world as a single woman. This would be new for me because I married my first boyfriend, and when that marriage was over, I met my second husband; I did not date other men before meeting either of them. This dating thing is all new territory to me! The fear of being alone was something else I had to deal with. The life that my husband and I had built would be no more. This was the more challenging thought: the dream of living happily ever after was over.

Admitting to myself that it was over was the hardest part of moving forward and the first step I needed to take. It was important to be honest with myself to be able to tell the truth to myself. I had lied to myself for years because I didn't want to believe that my life was falling apart. I had to come to a place where I was willing to redefine my story, my history from one of being a victim, a martyr, and a desperate housewife trying to save a relationship that was long over since long before I was willing to face it. I could not take one step without finding a reason to be happy, to find the woman that I had lost way before my failed marriages. I believe that this was very important to my process. This is when I started the emotional journey to self-worth. Three months into the process of writing this book it became apparent to me that this no longer was a healing journey for me alone, but an opportunity to share my experience with other woman who may feel that they are alone. I believe my story will show them that they are not alone and if I can make changes in my world then so can they. May my courage, encourage many.

I am willing to tell my truth as I perceived it. I now see the importance of telling my truth and being willing to put it all out there. I do this without shame or regret, for I could not share in this capacity if one thing from my past was different. There were moments in my life where the drama was overwhelming, humiliating and devastating. There was always some emotional hurdle to get over and after twenty plus years, I was exhausted and had no energy for hurdles anymore.

I see that this process has been a blessing that is yet to be completely revealed. I get to share my message of hope and inspiration to women from all walks of life. My story is no different from any other woman who has experienced low self-esteem, rejection, and the need for approval. It seems that this is the emotional makeup of a large part of the female population. I can only speak about what I've noticed in the media and its intended agenda to give girls a complex about themselves. How else can they sell their products without having you believe you need this or that to feel worthy? Once this is accomplished they then have you for life, that girl becomes a woman still looking outside herself for validation. It's designed to have women compare themselves to others, to question their beauty and what makes them uniquely beautiful. I had to find something more meaningful to fill the emptiness in my heart. I needed to discover what fulfills me and what makes me beautiful. I know that I feel beautiful doing something meaningful with my life, helping others by sharing my truth. The thought of being a public speaker and workshop facilitator, hosting weekend retreats for mothers and daughters, gives me such satisfaction. I know all that I have experienced has prepared me to be the best that I can be. It gives me more joy than I thought I could ever experience.

The most frequent question that I have been asked is "You seem so happy and content, how did you get here?"; it is a great question and I asked myself years ago, "What do I do and how do I do it? How do I get through this mentally and physically intact?" Above all for me is having an undeniable faith in God and the power of prayer, which has brought me to where I am today. When I was praying, this is the last place I thought I would be because I was praying for my husband to change and for him to be the man I wanted him to be. With that said, we as women, mothers and daughters must ultimately take responsibility for our emotional needs and ourselves. The spiritual part is huge but we still must take ownership over our lives, emotions, and how we choose to process things. When my second husband and I separated the first time, I felt as if someone had died, my mental state was not good and physically my body became weak and thin. I took sleeping pills at night and if needed, an anti-anxiety med during the day. My body was not being nourished and food had no taste or value to me anymore; I would force myself to eat. The children, who were 12, 14 and 24 at the time, were a mess as well, so all the way around it was not a good picture. I know from personal experience that the children are affected and if I am not my best self then what could I possibly give to my children? Remember, it is not possible to give what you don't have.

I allowed myself some time to just be numb and then knew I needed to get up and pull myself together, so that is what I did. Even though on the inside I was a disaster, looking at me from the outside I did not look so bad. I got ready each day, my hair, makeup, and a cute outfit. Not knowing each day what was to come, I at least looked prepared!

Before we separated we were in counseling at a wonderful place called The Healing House in Orlando, FL. The therapist we worked with at the time was a true-lifesaver for the children and I. She got us through some of the darkest days we had known as a family and to this day is someone I stay in touch with. A few years later, I found myself back at The Healing House seeing a different therapist, just trying to put together the pieces of me that I lost or checked out on years before. We were about to be empty nesters and I needed to find a purpose for Susan. I joined a women's group and we met every Tuesday, the power of women sharing from their hearts in a safe place facilitated by a therapist was invaluable to me. I began to take baby steps getting out of my comfort zone that I had created and I joined a charity and began practicing yoga, taking exercise seriously. For the first time in my life, I began true self-care to nourish my mind, body, and soul. I decided that I was going to make an honest effort at changing my life from the inside out. As it turned out, I wasn't only preparing to be an empty nester with our youngest moving out, but also a single woman living alone for the first time. The thought "what will I do with my life" turned out to be unfolding right before my eyes.

Over the years I had flirted with the idea of writing a book. I thought that some of my experiences were so out there that you just couldn't make it up. When possible, I dealt with my pain with humor. I thought at the very least that if I were to write a book that it would be entertaining. So this was the seed that was planted years before I was actually ready to write. Then I met a life-coach that reminded me that I had a great story to tell and that it would benefit women in more ways than I could imagine. I had no idea that this would set me on my path and purpose. This one decision has changed me and my family forever. I was being equipped to start a new life on my own and to end a marriage of 25 years.

So when I am asked "how did you do it?," the answer is slowly, purposefully, and one day at a time. I encourage women and men to seek help with people that they trust and feel safe in sharing their deepest truth. In this day and age, help is morethan just a phone call away. We now have the internet at our disposal. If we want it, it is available. There is an abundance of resources, people, and places to reach out to, you just have to be willing to do the research. Therapists, churches, books, spiritual healers, women's and men's groups, there is no limit as to what you can find when you are ready and willing.

You also have to be willing to let time pass because nothing happens overnight and nothing happens without pain and processing. You must find out what's going to be the thing to breathe life back into you and take the necessary steps to walk in that direction. Do not be afraid to tell someone. Do that and you have taken your first step to a new you. Then you will discover that you are worthy of the best that life has to offer and you will remember that you are worthy of a life partner that loves you as much as you love them. You will start to feel more free and confident in yourself and what you can do for your family.

FINAL THOUGHTS

Everyone has the opportunity to teach by example, by being the woman you were meant to be! As we stand in our authenticity we inspire others that there is more to be lived, that they can do the same. If you are honest you will see yourself in my story and more importantly, may you find the courage, as I have done, to do something to make your life better and to tell your own story.

Made in the USA
Charleston, SC
16 December 2016